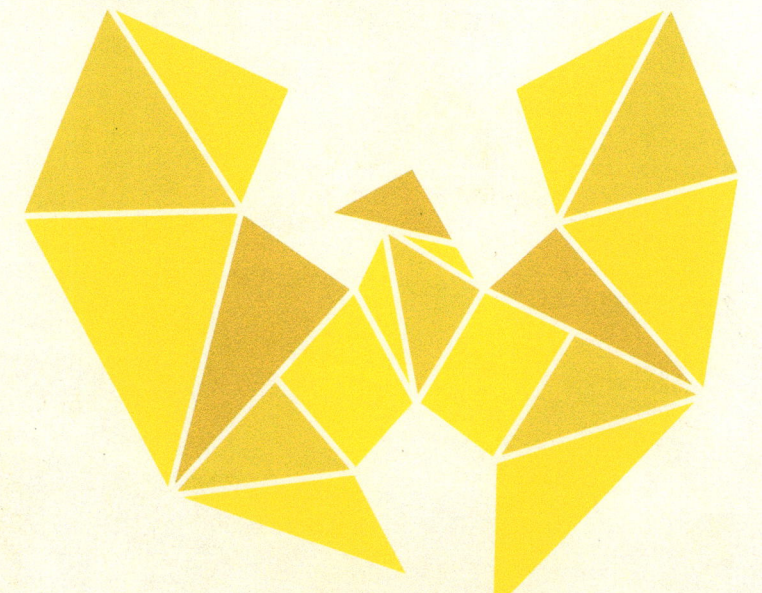

WUIKU
ENTER THE 36TH CHAMBER

Written & Designed By - André S. Pope & Brenden R. Goodcuff
Edited By - Dean Blumberg | Photographer - Bobby Altman

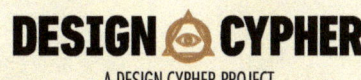

A DESIGN CYPHER PROJECT

Copyright © 2017 – Design Cypher, LLC

All rights reserved. This book or any portion thereof may not be reproduced or used in any manner whatsoever without the express written permission of the publisher except for the use of brief quotations in a book review or scholarly journal.

First Printing: 2017
ISBN-13: 978-1977538781
ISBN-10: 197753878X

Design Cypher, LLC
Conway, South Carolina
www.thedesigncypher.com
info@thedesigncypher.com

DEDICATION

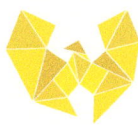

Dedicated to the winners and the losers. Dedicated to all Jeeps and Land Cruisers.

This is dedicated to all of the educators (teachers, parents, community leaders) working to make a difference, seeing potential where others dismissed it, and lifting up their community, one pupil at a time.

While most of society may not notice, the few individuals you connect with do.

"Real people do real things."

André S. Pope – "The Professor"

Dedicated to Professor Pope for always pushing me in the right direction with design, and to Carly for pretty much doing the same with everything else.

Brenden Goodcuff – "14KT GOLD SLUM COMPUTER WIZARD"

Shaolin SLUM
NO EXIT →

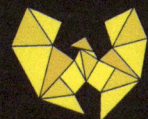

TABLE OF CONTENTS

6. INTRODUCTION: André Pope —
   A.K.A. *The Professor*
7. INTRODUCTION: Brenden Goodcuff —
   A.K.A. *The 14kt Gold Slum Computer Wizard*
8. FINDING WAYS TO CONNECT
9. WUIKU COVER ART

TRACK LISTING

10. Bring da Ruckus
12. Shame on a Nigga
14. Clan in da Front
16. Wu-Tang: 7th Chamber
18. Can It Be All So Simple / Intermission
20. Da Mystery of Chessboxin'
22. Wu-Tang Clan Ain't Nuthing ta F' Wit
24. C.R.E.A.M.
26. Method Man
28. Protect Ya Neck
30. Tearz

THE PROFESSOR

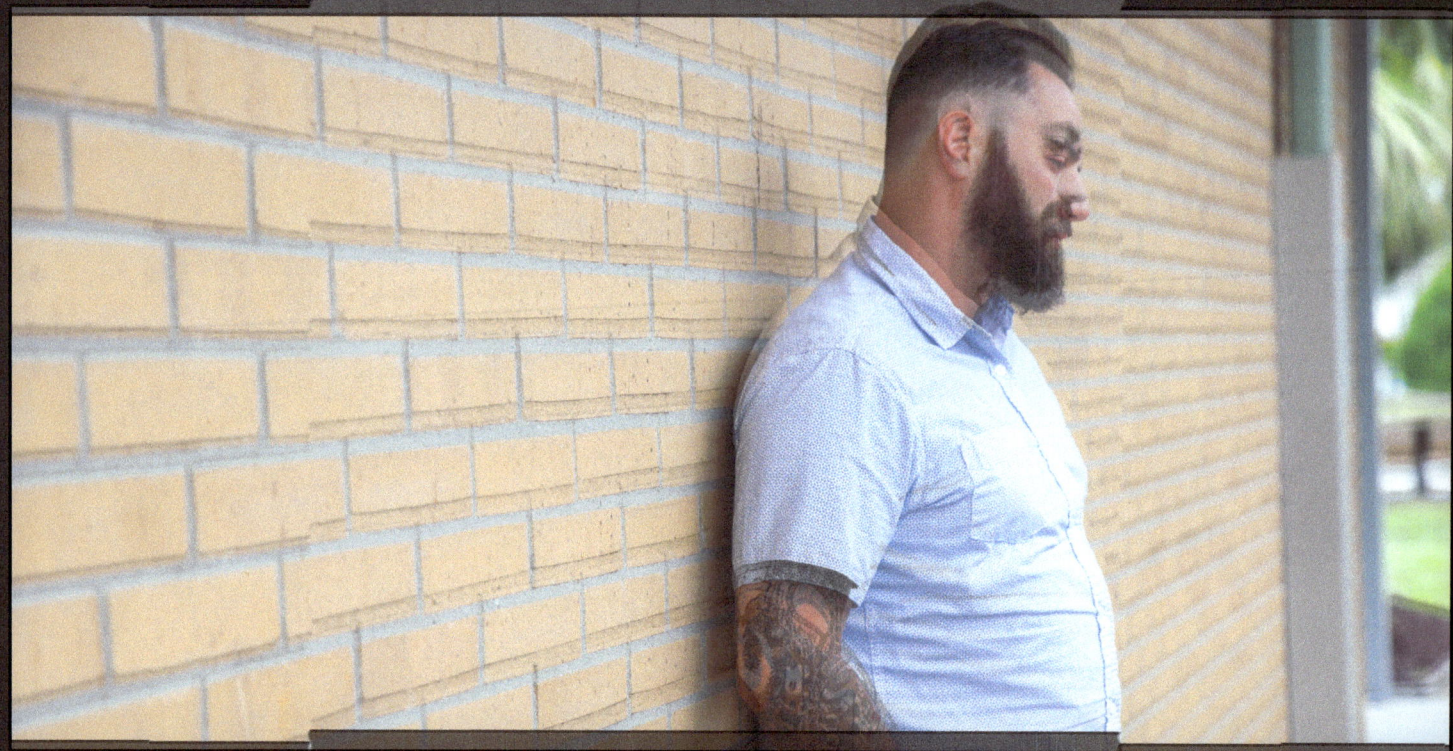

André S. Pope — A.K.A. The Professor, was born in Owensboro, KY in March of 1980 and raised on a family farm outside Conway, SC. Raised by his father, Pope was brought up in a house where "Beach Music" — The Tams, The Platters, The Drifters — was in heavy rotation.

While other children were spinning pop tunes, Pope was trading Metallica's *Black Album* for a cassette of Ice T's *Original Gangster*. This unlikely pairing would set a precedent that would influence Pope for years to come.

At 18, Pope sought refuge from small-town farm life, moving to New York City and attending New York University for Graphic Communications. During his time at NYU, Pope was receiving another sort of education in the city. After seeing Run DMC at the legendary club Tramps and attending crappy punk shows at CBGB's, Pope was getting an undergraduate lesson in how a "DIY" scene culture really took shape.

Although he left NYU for The Art Institutes of Atlanta a year later, the grassroots hardcore and hip-hop scenes of NYC would prove more influential than he'd imagine. After receiving his degree and carving out his own little niche in advertising design and brand identity, Pope's passion turned into entrepreneurial spirit with the formation of his first company. Pope, along with his business partners, took the DIY lifestyle to a whole new level, growing the company from its humble beginnings in one of his partner's kitchens, to the back of a surf shop, to a full-fledge office, to being acquired by another local business.

Today, Pope finds himself back in the classroom as a digital arts professor at a local technical college. He wants students and local area talent to be exposed to some of the richness that he experienced in his time in NYC — the youthful idealism of a DIY hardcore scene, the sharp wits of a rhyme on a boom-bap beat, the energy of life in art.

14KT GOLD SLUM COMPUTER WIZARD

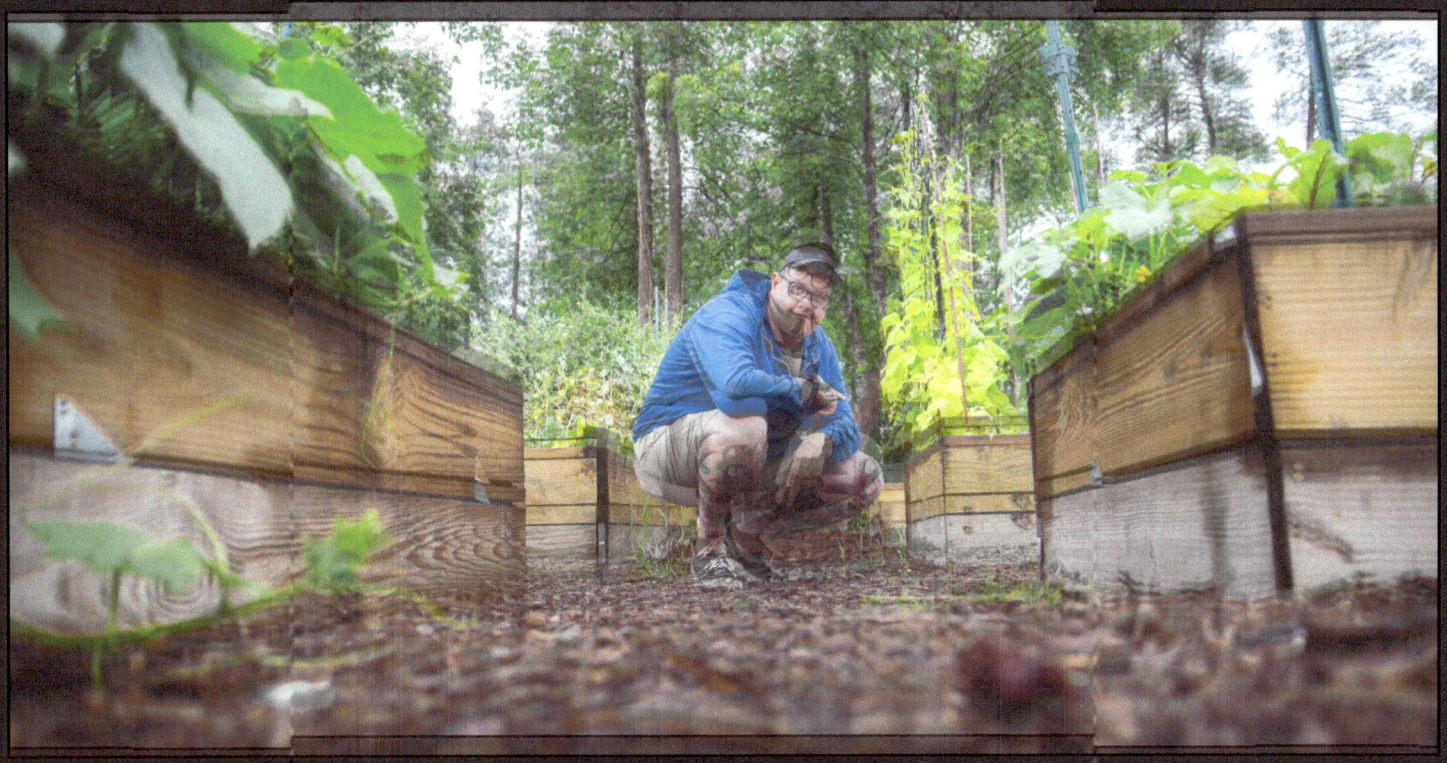

Brenden Goodcuff — A.K.A. The 14kt Gold Slum Computer Wizard, was born in Westchester County, New York in July of 1990. Around the age of 5 his family moved to Surfside Beach, SC where Brenden lived a pretty normal suburban beach life. While he didn't fit in with the typical flip-flop, popped collar, Croakies crowd, Brenden sought refuge in his own creative endeavors.

In 10th grade, after receiving a bootleg copy of Fruity Loops, the digital audio creator, Brenden began his own sonic experiments. Discovering Nas' deftly lyrical *Illmatic* and Wu-Tang Clan's gritty and raw *Enter the Wu-Tang* helped combat the ennui and despair of the institutional public school system that was quickly stifling Brenden's creative nature. He took to music production and soon was creating beats for local hip-hop acts.

After high school, Brenden enrolled at the local technical college and decided to pursue graphic design. Brenden put his creative design skills to work crafting merch and flyers for punk and hardcore bands. Discouraged with a lack of community at school, Brenden dropped out, only to find that flippin' burgers doesn't have much of a future. Luckily, during his second attempt at college, Brenden met Professor Pope in the digital arts department.

Brenden appreciated Pope's "direct from the industry" approach to design and education. Experiencing design first-hand by being included in real world advertising scenarios clicked with Brenden. Pope's no-nonsense, but don't-take-yourself-too-seriously approach to design was refreshing.

Brenden began to excel at the design process. After winning two "Addy Awards" from the American Federation of Graphic Design, Brenden looked for tutelage outside the classroom. Brenden and Pope once again connected, and their mutual love for hardcore and rap birthed the Wuiku project.

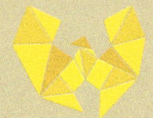

FINDING WAYS TO CONNECT

Music is a common denominator that connects us. It allows us to understand, relate, and share an unspoken bond. Often, it is all you need to unveil the great potential that exists in all of us.

Music was the common ground needed to transform former college drop-out Brenden Goodcuff to a star student with unbridled potential.

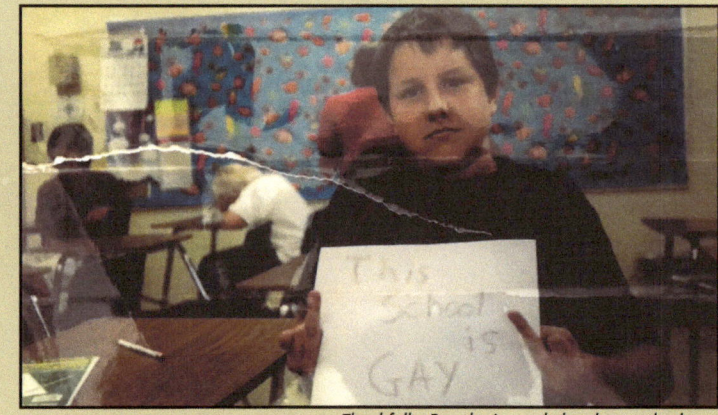

Thankfully, Brenden's vocabulary has evolved too.

The 1992 release of Wu-Tang Clan's *Enter the Wu-Tang (36 Chambers)* was the spark that united Professor Pope and Mr. Goodcuff. The gritty nature of the album and an awe-inspiring rhyme flow immediately resonated with both Professor Pope and Mr. Goodcuff. For Pope, it was during his early teenage years when he was coping with being a caucasian hip-hop kid in a small southern town. For Mr. Goodcuff, he experienced *Enter the Wu-Tang (36 Chambers)* as he dug through crates trying to connect with hip-hop's past. While they both experienced the album at different times in their lives, it nonetheless had an everlasting and profound effect.

In the graphic design classroom, Pope used *Enter the Wu-Tang (36 Chambers)* as a tool for communication and understanding with Goodcuff. Breaking out of the mold of traditional design, Pope and Goodcuff collaborated on a cypher-style process of design. A project was born between professor and student to look at ways of incorporating art, design, music, and poetry beyond the classroom:

"Wuiku - Enter the 36th Chamber"

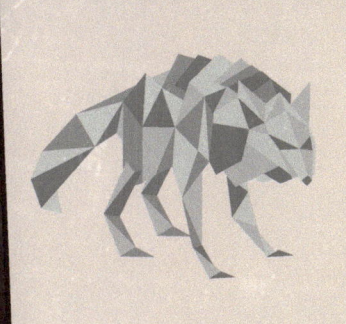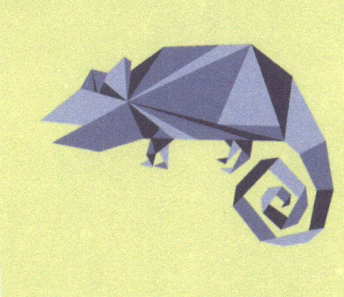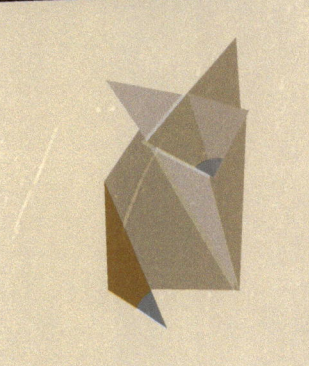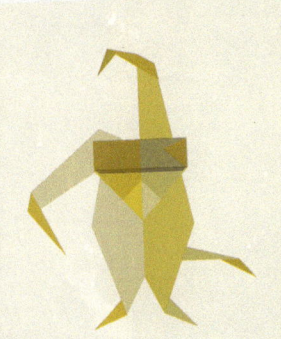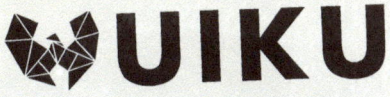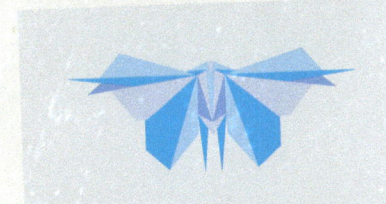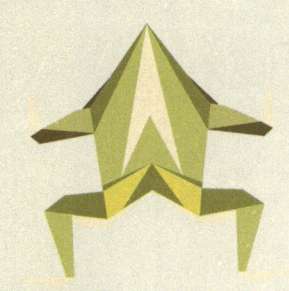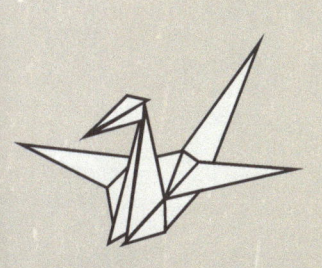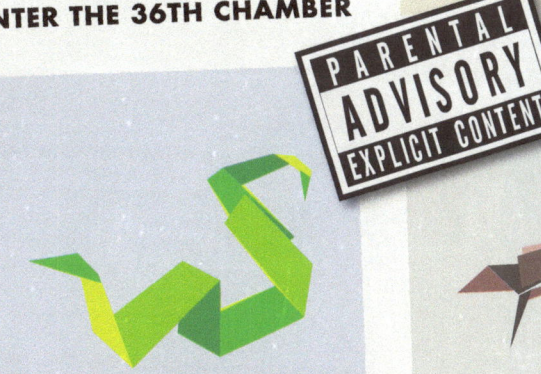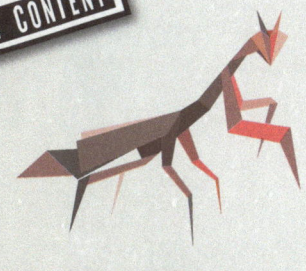

UIKU

ENTER THE 36TH CHAMBER

PARENTAL ADVISORY EXPLICIT CONTENT

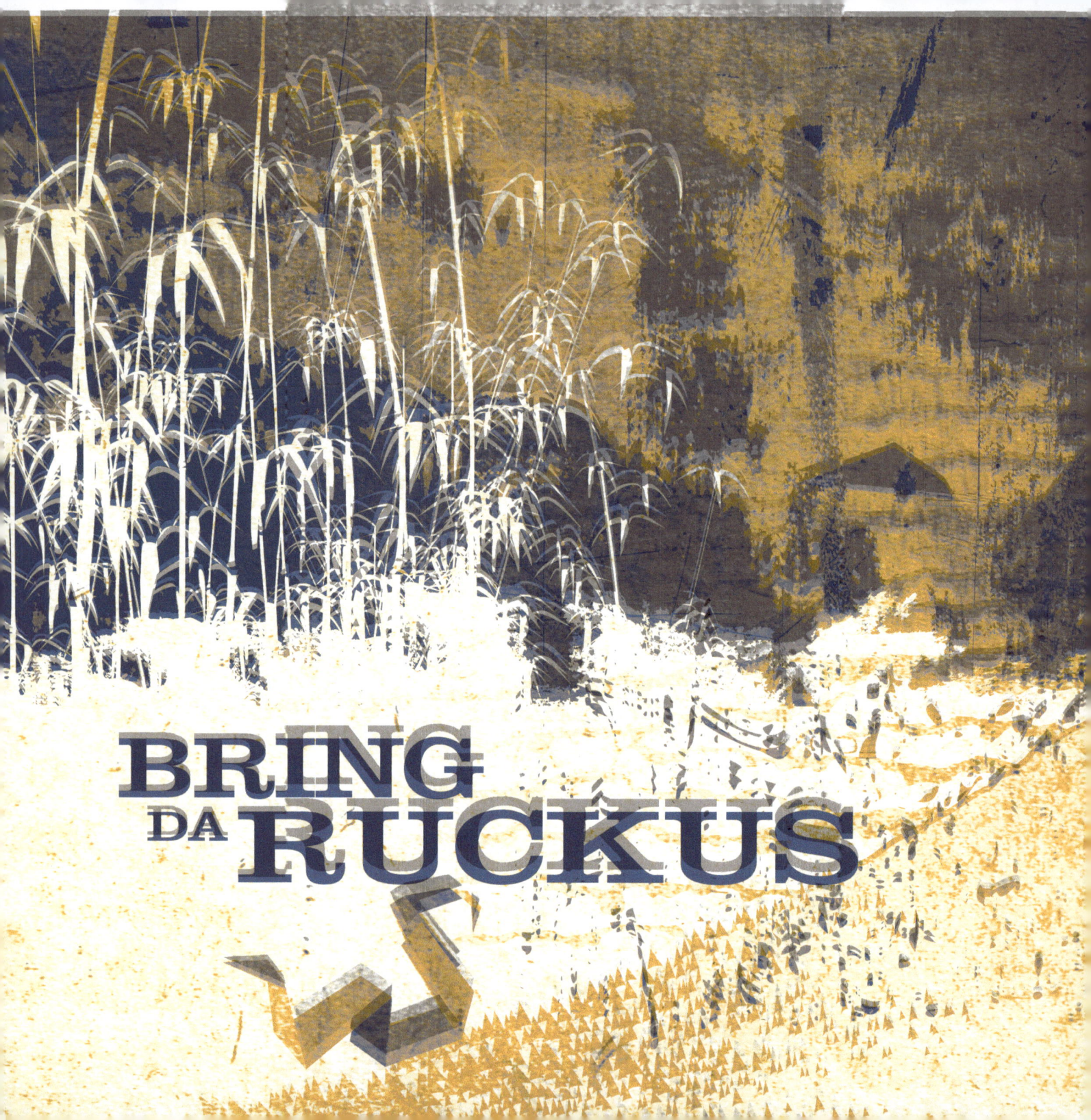

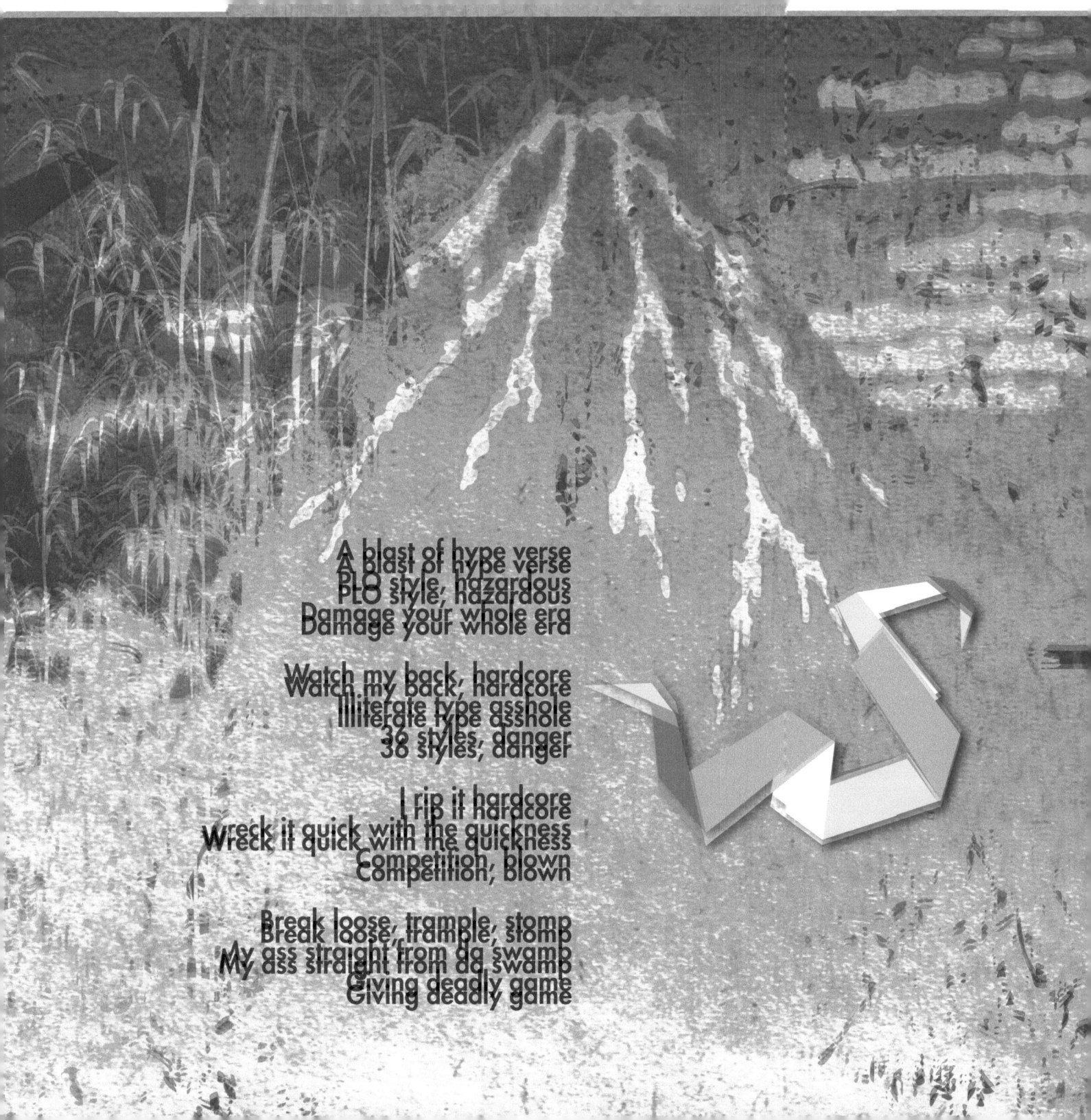

A blast of hype verse
PLO style, hazardous
Damage your whole era

Watch my back, hardcore
Illiterate type asshole
36 styles, danger

I rip it hardcore
Wreck it quick with the quickness
Competition, blown

Break loose, trample, stomp
My ass straight from da swamp
Giving deadly game

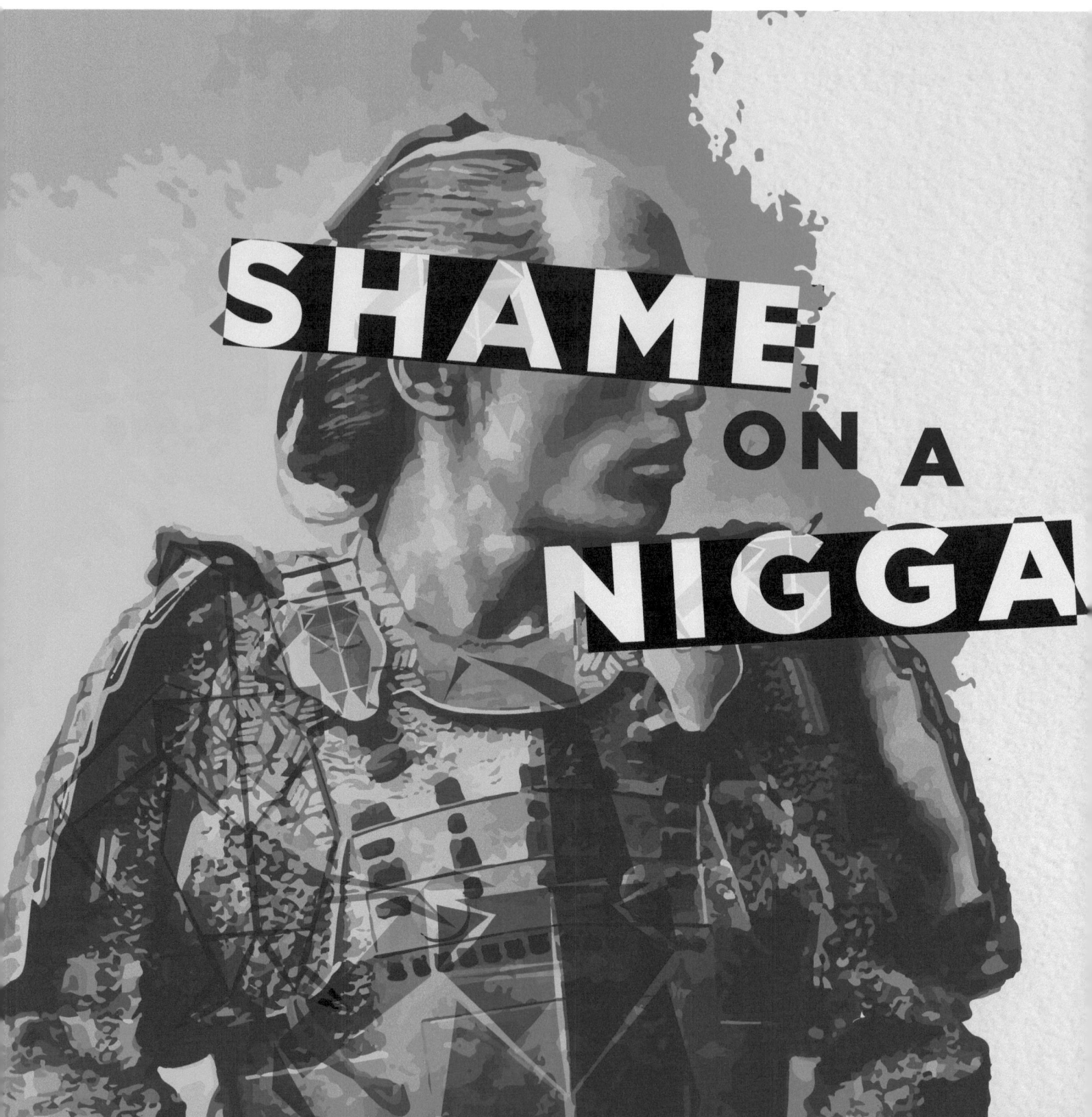

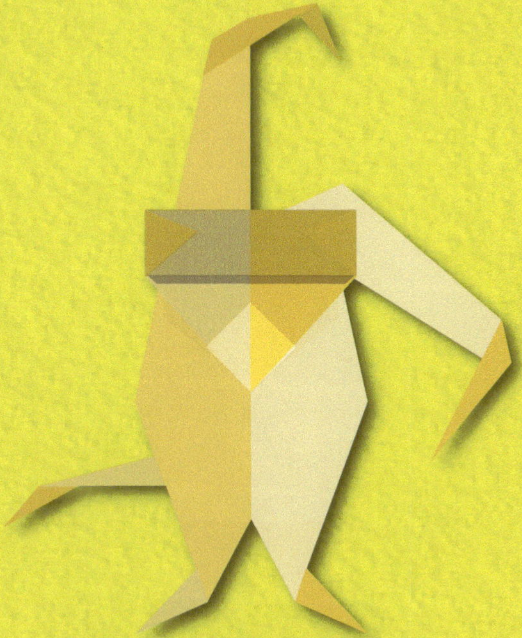

Buck wild the tiger
Try to run game, nigga
I'll fuck ya ass up

Do not fuck the style
Unbreakable, shatterproof
How you like me now?

My clan, understand
We gunning, coming at ya
Razor sharp, sever

React so thick
Brothers approach and half step
Ain't heard half it yet

Like a house on fire
Taste the flame of the Wu-Tang
Tiger vs. Crane

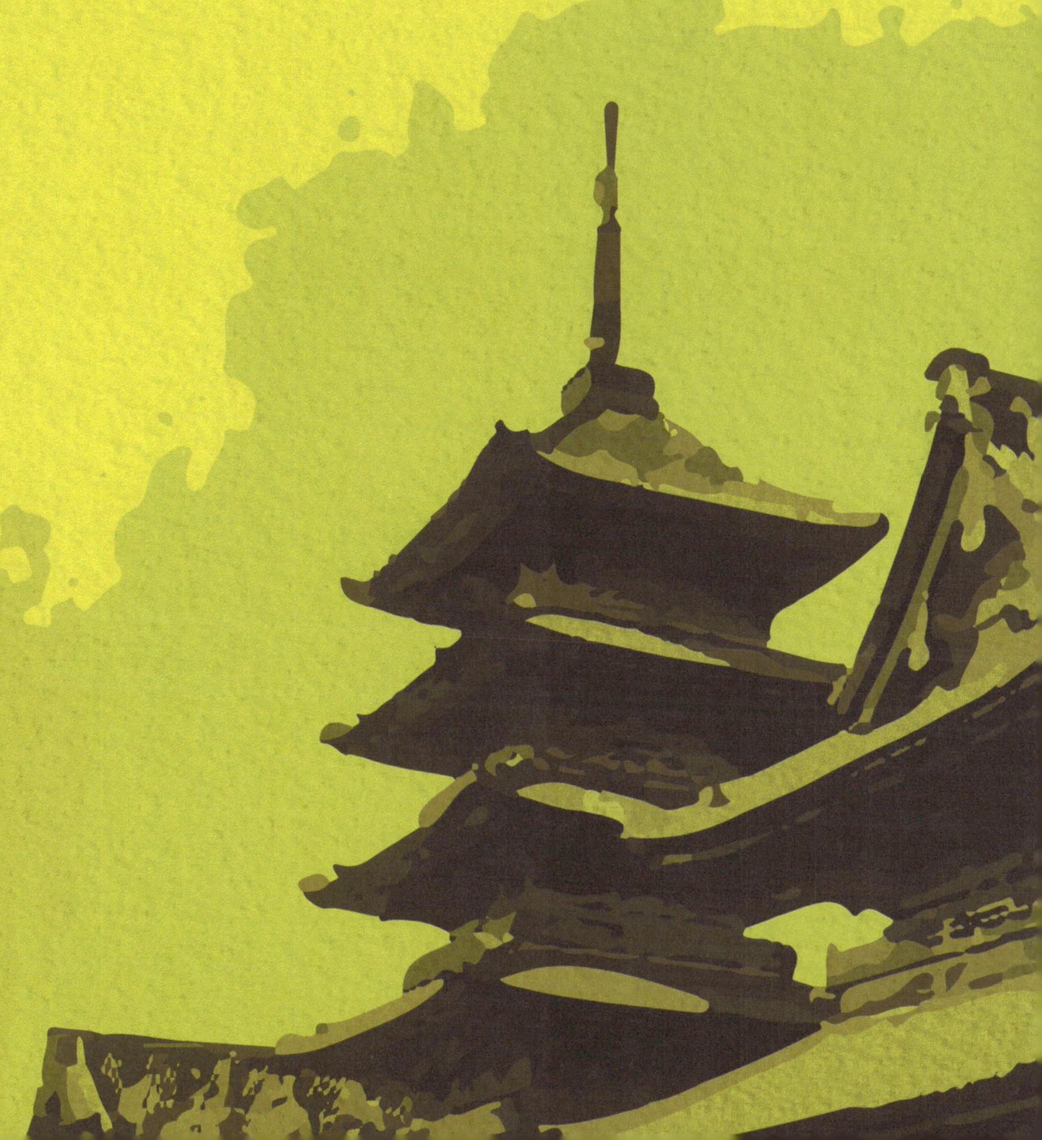

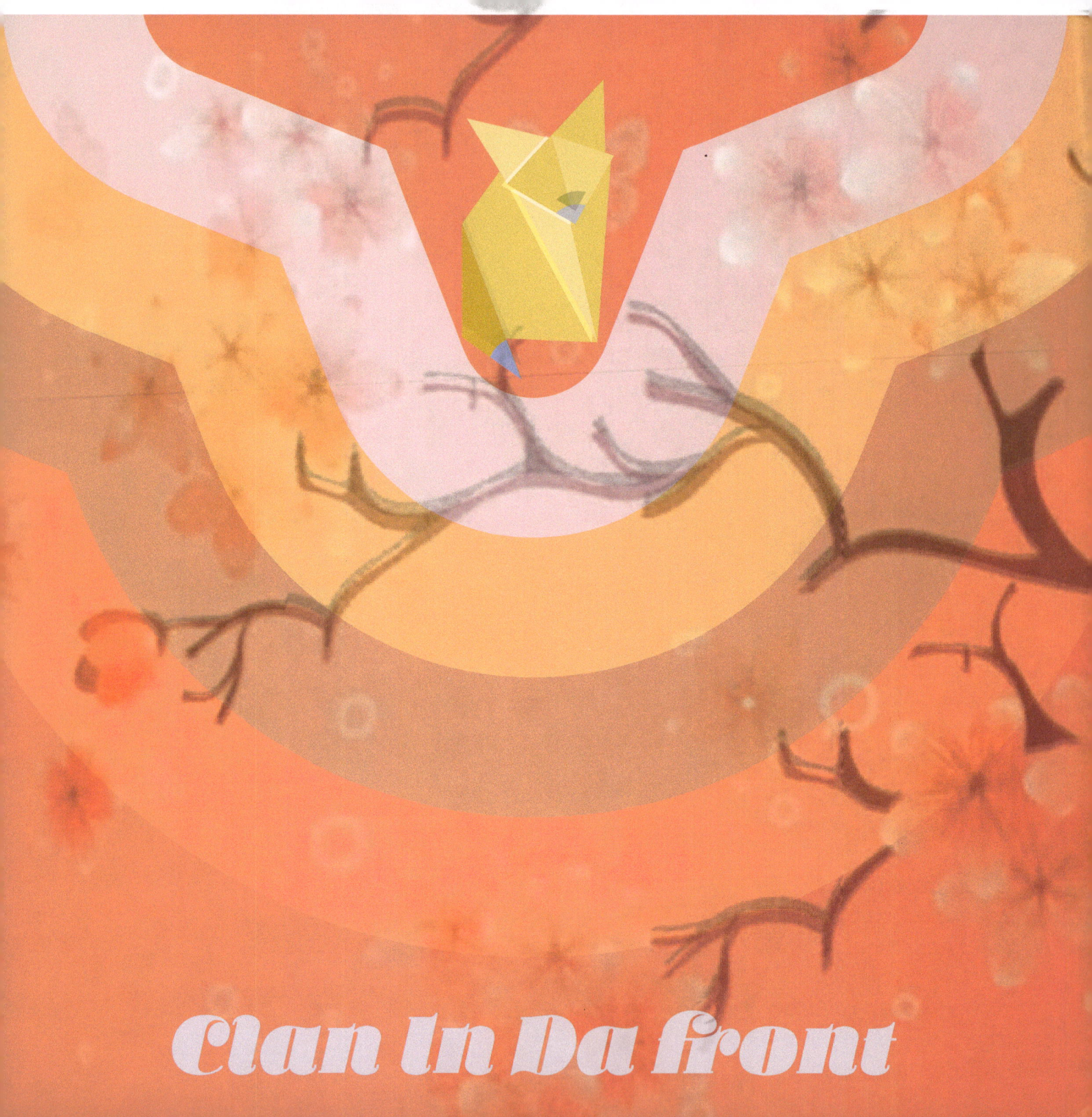

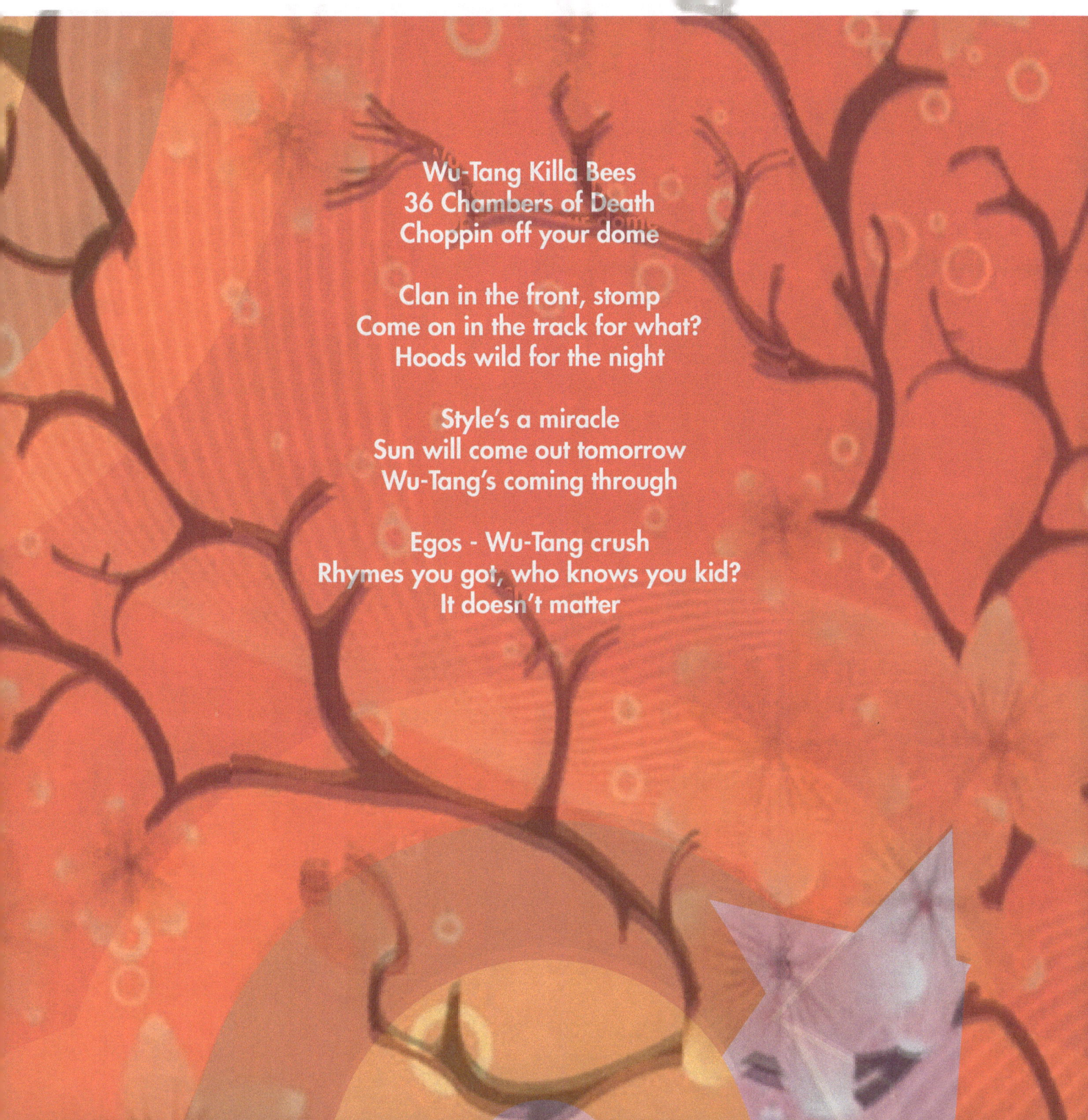

Wu-Tang Killa Bees
36 Chambers of Death
Choppin off your dome

Clan in the front, stomp
Come on in the track for what?
Hoods wild for the night

Style's a miracle
Sun will come out tomorrow
Wu-Tang's coming through

Egos - Wu-Tang crush
Rhymes you got, who knows you kid?
It doesn't matter

7TH CHAMBER

Hardcore, giving more
Raw sound, going to war now
My beats break you down

Hit me with that shit
Yo, this is my show, tical
Buddha monks with owls

Murderous madman,
The mic wrecker, Inspector
You dare to compare?

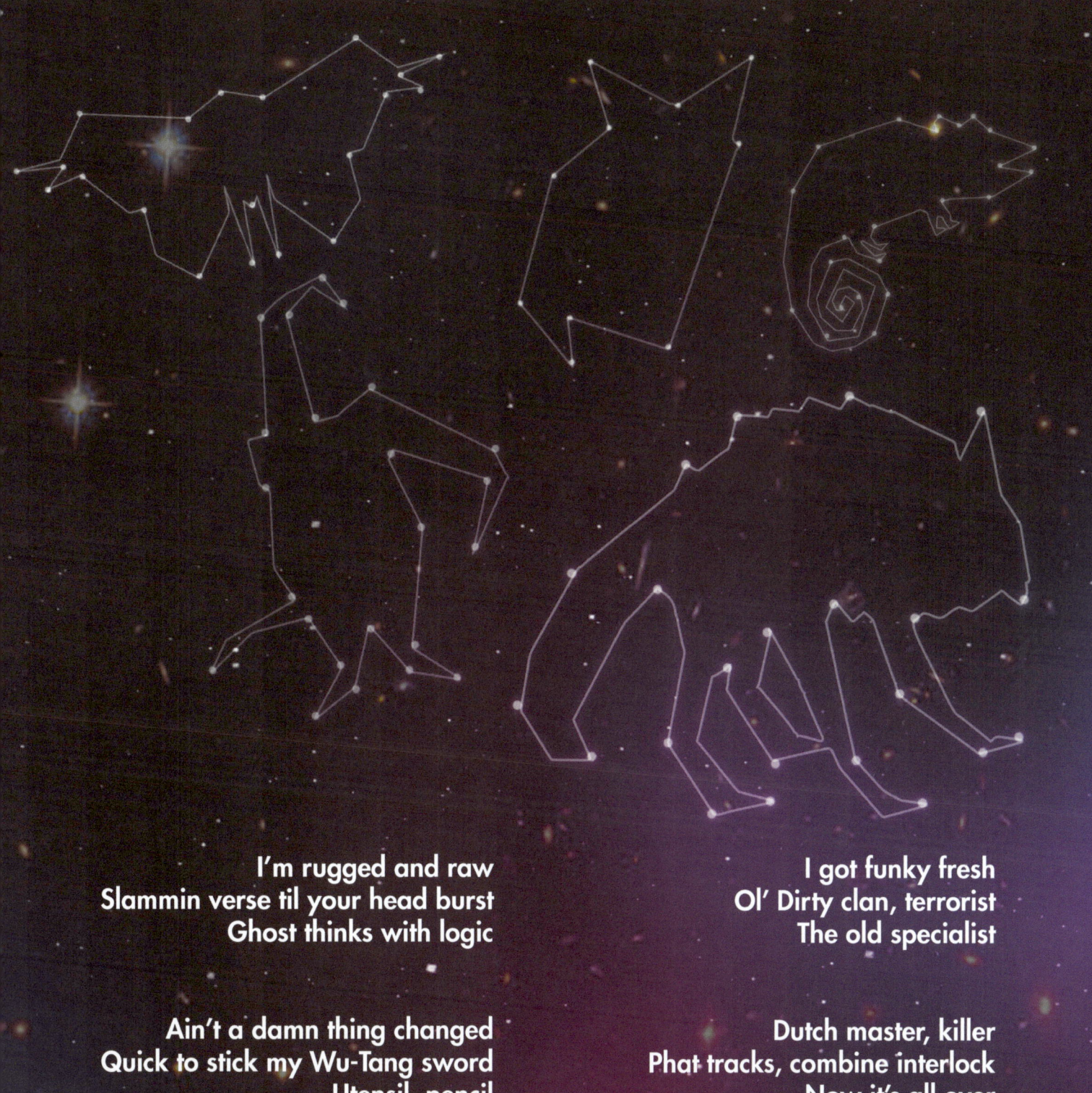

I'm rugged and raw
Slammin verse til your head burst
Ghost thinks with logic

I got funky fresh
Ol' Dirty clan, terrorist
The old specialist

Ain't a damn thing changed
Quick to stick my Wu-Tang sword
Utensil, pencil

Dutch master, killer
Phat tracks, combine interlock
Now it's all over

CAN IT BE ALL SO SIMPLE

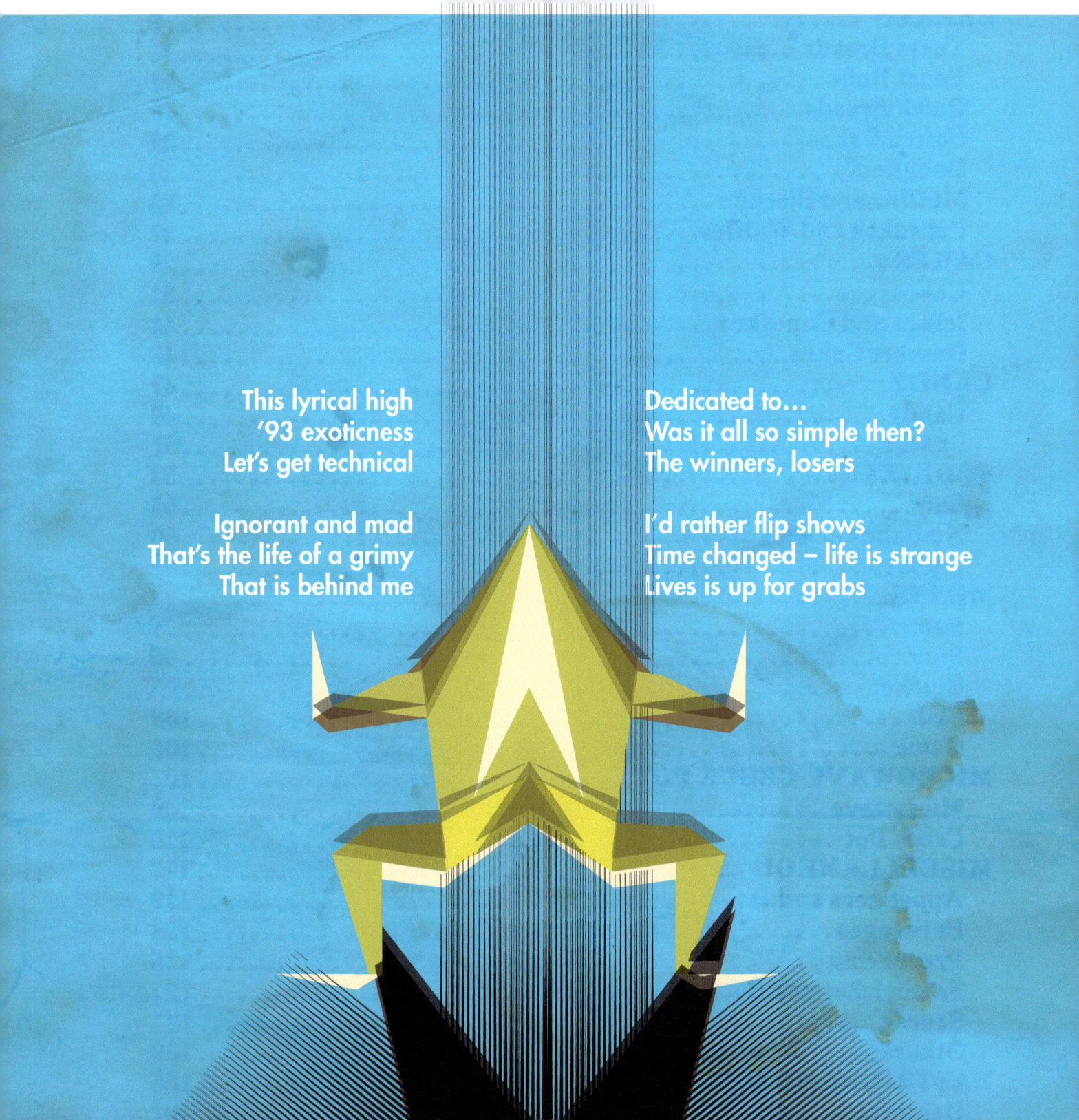

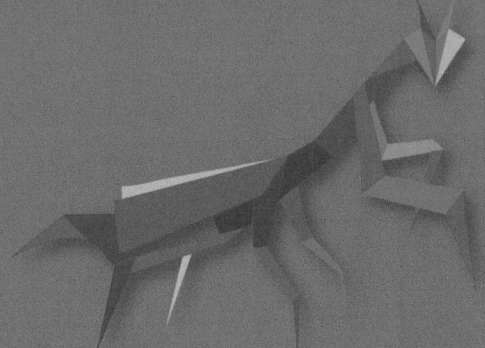

DA MYSTERY OF CHESSBOXIN'

Hip-hop, rock and shock
You might as well bang your head
My force you're doubting

From the Shaolin slum
Phony niggas outlined in chalk
There's no surviving

Rough like Timberland
I got to get my props, win it
Got beef with gold teeth

Peoples, where you at?
The killa bees on attack
Hitting cats with gats

Getting low with flow
Get up and be somebody
Ol' Dirty type slang

Yo, nobody budge
I killed you in a past life
Get the shit right, son

The mantis rapture
Merciless, hard to capture
Work of a master

Wu-Tang Clan Ain't Nuthing ta F' Wit

No place to hide
Fatal, flying guillotine
The Wu-Tang shogun

Needle to the groove
Slam tracks like quarterback sacks
I earth slam the best

And if you want beef
Wu ain't nuttin to fuck with
Better bring the ruckus

A fork in the road
Which way to go? Just follow
Rather do than die

Nuttin to fuck wit
Peace to all the gods and earths
It ain't safe no more

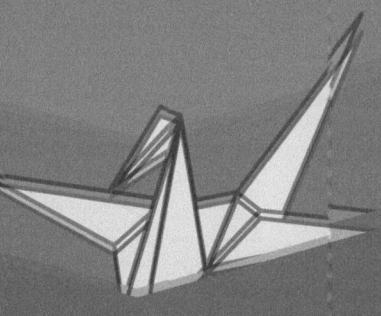

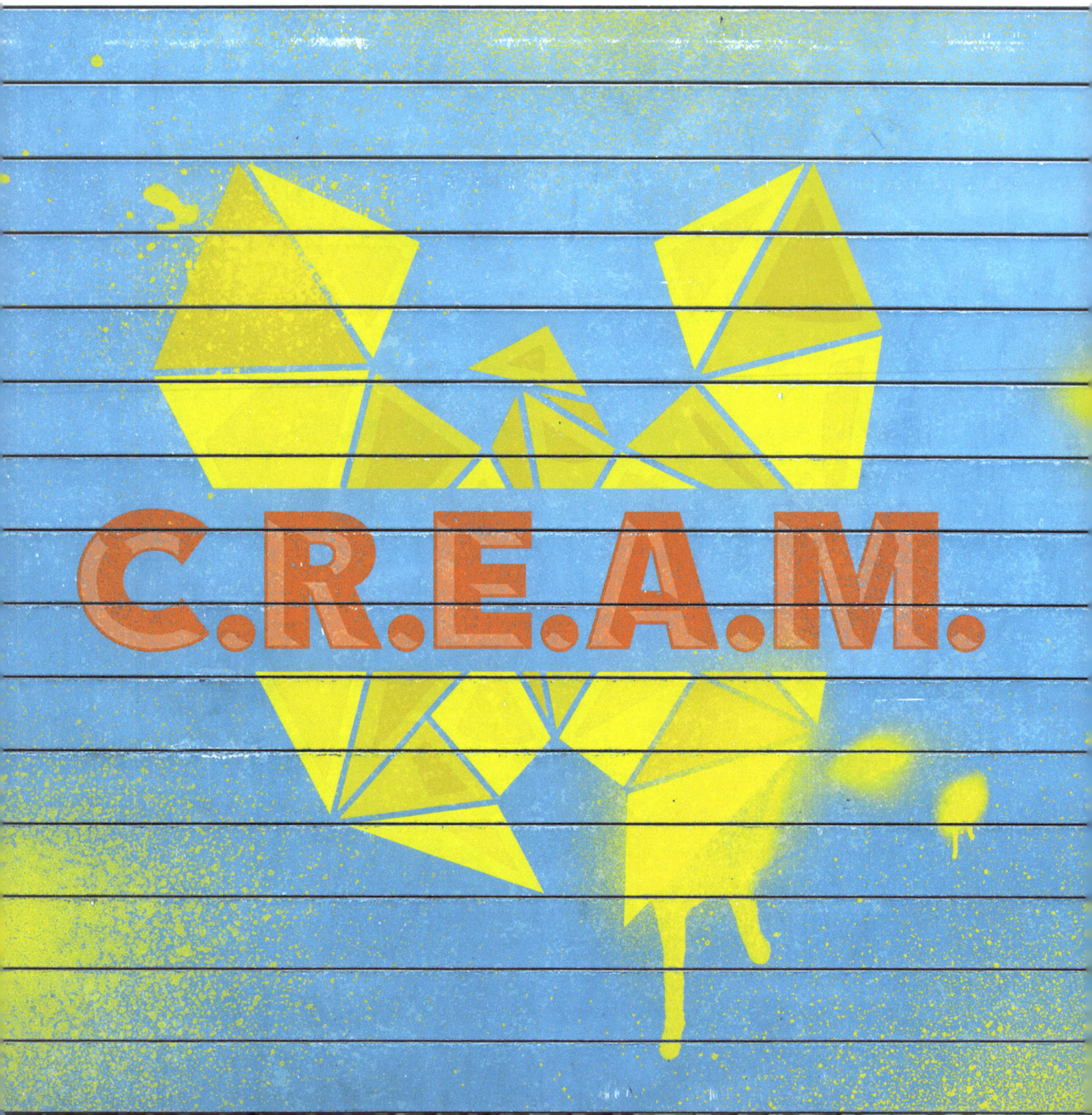

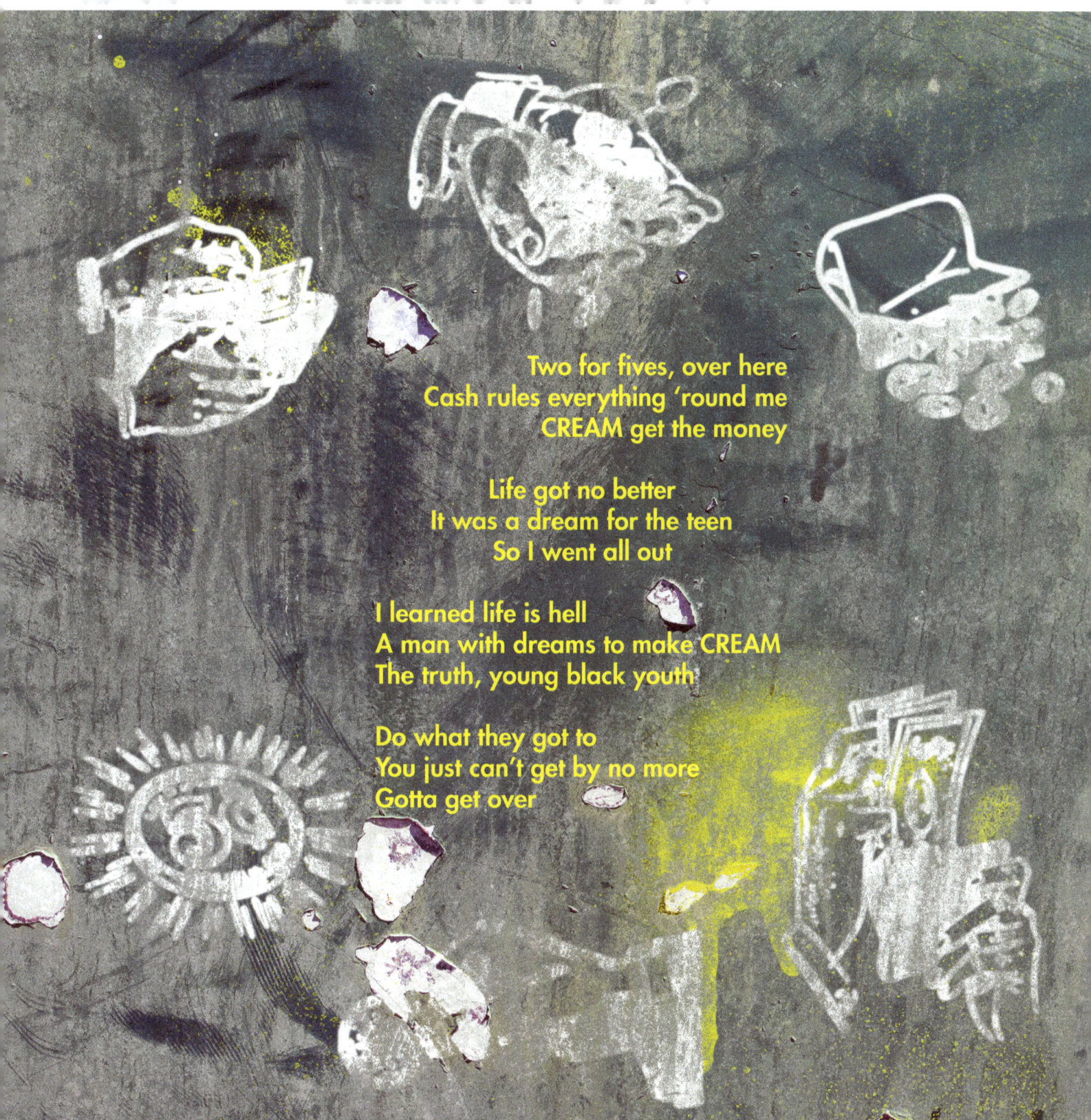

Two for fives, over here
Cash rules everything 'round me
CREAM get the money

Life got no better
It was a dream for the teen
So I went all out

I learned life is hell
A man with dreams to make CREAM
The truth, young black youth

Do what they got to
You just can't get by no more
Gotta get over

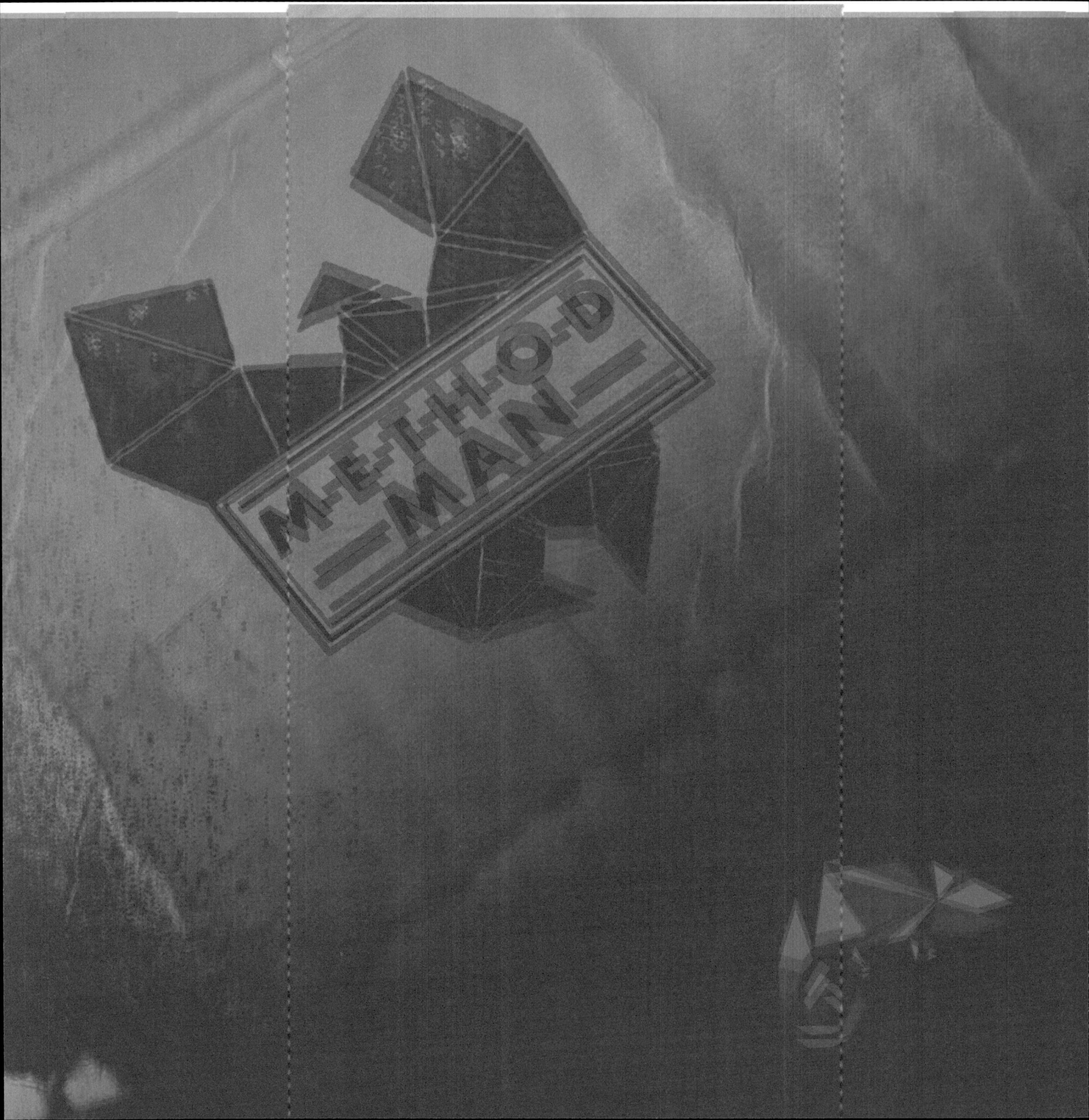

Oh shit that's the jam
Hitting from every angle
Ain't no average flow

I get bags of skunk
About to go get lifted
We do it like this

The cold wind's blowin
Savior or major flavor
Freak, flow, fancy free

I smoke on the mic
The art to rip charts apart
Too hot to handle

Make the crowd go wild
The rap assassinator
With the thoughts that bomb

It's the Method Man
And set it off, get it off
I wanna break fool

Grab my nut get screwed
Oww, here comes my Shaloin style
My crew with a "suuue"

When you step through to
I'm straight from the Brooklyn Zoo
Dirty and stinking

Ejecting styles from...
My pen, my lethal weapon
Point-blank, there it goes

Feeling mad hostile,
Like when I speaks the gospel
Ruckus, buck us style

Like Cain did Abel
You misuse what I invent
You lose every cent

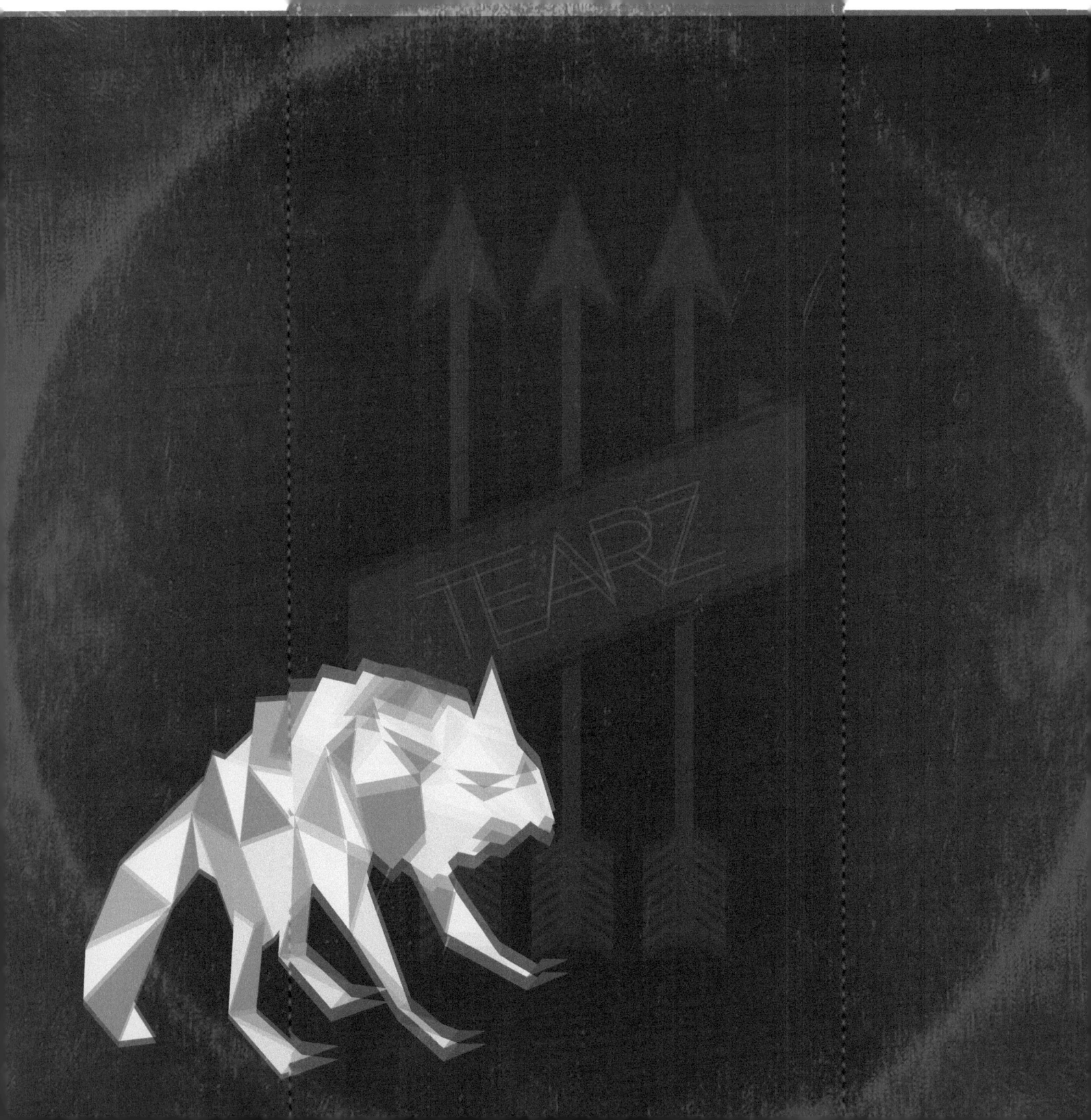

God's getting ripped
Brothers began to discuss
How to say goodbye?

Down with O.P.P.
Not worth it to go raw deal
Caught with H.I.V.

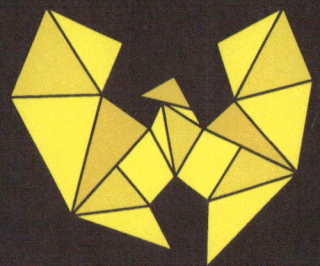

Wu-Tang Clan is: Prince Rakeem "The Rza", The Method Man, U-God, Rebel INS, Shallah Raekwon, Ghost Face Killer, Ol' Dirty Bastard, and The Genius "The Gza"

All Songs -
Written by the Wu-Tang Clan
Produced, Mixed and Arranged by Prince Rakeem "The Rza" for Wu-Tang Productions
"Da Mystery of Chessboxin'" – Co-Produced by Ol' Dirty Bastard
"Wu-Tang Clan Ain't Nuthing Ta F' Wit" – Co-Produced by The Method Man
Engineered by Ethan Ryman, except "Da Mystery of Chessboxin" engineered by Carlos Bess
Recorded & Mixed at Firehouse Studio, NY, NY
Scratches by the 4th Disciple
Programmed by Prince Rakeem
Edited at GLC, NYC
Mastered by Chris Gehringer at The Hit Factory, NYC

Can It Be All So Simple: Excerpts from *"The Way We Were"* performed by Gladys Knight and The Pips, used courtesy of Essex Entertainment. Written by Alan Bergman/Marilyn Bergman/Marvin Hamlisch. Published by Colgems-EMI Music Inc. (ASCAP); C.R.E.A.M.: Excerpts from *"As Long As I've Got You"* performed by the Charmels, used courtesy of Warner Special Products. Written by Isaac Hayes/David Porter. Published by Irving Music Inc. (BMI), TEARZ: Excerpts from *"After Laughter (Comes Tears)"* performed by Wendy Rene, used courtesy of Warner Special Products. Written by Johnnie Frierson/Mary Frierson. Published by Irving Music Inc. (BMI)

Executive Producers: Robert Diggs, Oli Grant, Mitchell Digs, Dennis Coles
Production Supervisors: Mitchell Digs, Oli Grant, John Gibbons, Theodore Michael, Mike McDonald
Wu-Tang Management: John Gibbons, Mike McDonald, Mitchell Diggs, John Hamilton, Jonathan Lugo, Vince Hamlin
A&R Direction (Loud Records): Trevor Williams
Published by Wu-Tang Publishing (BMI)

www.ingramcontent.com/pod-product-compliance
Lightning Source LLC
Chambersburg PA
CBHW051938210526
45473CB00006B/2297